Solidarity

FINDING SOLIDARITY IN HEARTBREAK, DEPRESSION & ANXIETY

BY: LYNN MOORE
@CUPOFTEAPOETRY

To the family and friends who were there to pick up the pieces.

Solidarity

I now intimately know strangers
Recognize the agony in their eyes
See the grief behind their well-placed smiles
Our situations may be different
But our hearts ache the same
Mirrored battles in our brains
We're all doing the best we can
I applaud our strength
Putting one foot in front of the other
Even when you want to stop
I want to cheer for us
We're doing it, despite all odds
Life keeps on moving, but so do we
Soldiers in our own invisible battle
Trying to make it through another day
It helps to know I'm not alone
Other people are hurting too
There's solidarity in pain

REFLECTIONS

Cinderella Complex

The most dangerous sentence you can tell a young girl
And they lived happily ever after
Every book, every movie, reinforces the lie
We're hardwired to love, to need, to be completed
Waiting in a tower for our knight in shining armor
To save us

Depending on a man to make us whole
Teaching us that we weren't complete to begin with
A man is the final piece to our puzzle
True love's kiss will break the spell

As we grow up, we devour romance in all of its forms
We sing along to love songs
Stay up late with butterflies turning page after page
Falling in love with fictional characters
Not realizing the damage we're doing
Until it's too late

We enter relationships and expect forever
Each person is prince charming, our perfect ending
The fairy tales tell us to go all-in
It all works out in the end
Happily ever after is right at our fingertips

We expect the perfect story, but that never happens
Our relationships to play out like a romantic comedy
But we never see the full story
What happens behind the scenes
The fights, the imperfections
The bumps along the way
We hide our own struggles
Behind photoshopped smiles fishing for likes

Have blind faith in those who don't deserve it
And get hurt again and again
When the end comes, we're blindsided
After putting all of our faith into love
We're left depleted

Believing in a fabrication programmed into our brains
Instead of pouring our energy
Into a career and ourselves
We try to turn the beast into the prince
Putting their needs before our own
We're the caretakers
The supporting character in the story

While little boys are told to be knights and warriors
Little girls are given toys
With unrealistic proportions
Taught how to be obedient
And press play on stories that focus on romance
As if that's all that girls need to hear
Every story ends with a kiss

Why are you surprised when we earn less
Are pushed aside?
When from day one you've taught us
To be a damsel in distress
Trained to dream of the perfect man
Not the perfect job

Besides falling in love and starting a family
What should we want?
Society tells us that's all that we need
The perfect recipe for happiness

Once it's taken away and we're left with nothing
No backup plan
No leading man to whisk us away into the sunset
We finally realize the answer all along
We have to save ourselves
No one is coming to rescue us
We're the heroes of our own stories

Throw away the Disney fairytales
Push pause on the RomCom
Push play on the documentary
Close the romance novel, open the autobiography
Breathe in tales of powerful women

Dream of your own adventures
Create your own success
Any partner that comes into the picture
Is just your supporting character
Meant to add to your life, not become it

Tipped Scales

You wanted someone that would never leave
Holding all the cards in your hands
I was just an innocent bystander
Caught up in your spell, I had no choice
Blinded by your light
I'd follow you anywhere
Your love was cursed
I willingly gave up my power
Thinking I won the lottery
Everything I ever wanted
Delivered in a dangerously beautiful box
You needed the upper hand
To avoid getting hurt
The scales always tipped in your favor
Everyone said I was so lucky to have you
I didn't see the imbalance
Couldn't read between the lines
Gave you all of my heart, everything I had
But in the back of your mind
You wanted more
I would never be enough
So you had to cut your losses
And walk away

Shattered

I remember the day I realized
We weren't guaranteed forever
You could change your mind
Something could happen
The security I felt exploded
Naked and terrified
I asked for reassurance
Which you gave in the best way you could
Glued my pieces back together
How do people live like this?
Knowing the other person could walk away
At any time, for any reason
One day I would wake up alone
My realization turned into a premonition
A few months later
You chose to walk away
I shattered again
But this time you weren't there
To put back the pieces

Seamstress

I threaded you into the seams of my life
You were the vital colors
Making the picture complete
A permanent fixture
You couldn't remove the thread
Without ruining the art
I didn't see the frays
Until you ripped the stitches
As gently as possible
You needed the thread
To sew something new
A different picture
With a better artist

Comparisions

We live in a virtual reality
Filled with beauty and perfection
Photoshopped bodies and perfect
features
We're sold an artificial
attractiveness
Not naturally attainable
Very few come out of the box flawless
It takes work and money
Personal trainers and boutique
fitness classes
Diets so clean they're sterile
People paid to be beautiful
And in shape
Thigh gaps and six-packs
The average person can't compete
We try to work with what we have
Scrolling past people
Way more beautiful
With better style, better looks,
A better canvas
Slowly we beat ourselves down
Hating the face in the mirror
Staring back at us
Wishing it would change
Always disappointed

Can I Please Be Her?

I want to be the girl who wears
Crop tops and yoga pants
Effortlessly beautiful without makeup
Thigh gap and abs on display
Knows where to get the best matcha
Shops at the farmer's market
Always carries a reusable water bottle
Reads feminist books in the park
Works from coffee shops
Plenty of money in the bank
Brunches with her group of girlfriends
Takes high-end pilates and spin classes
Hikes with her well-behaved dog off-leash
Travels to beautiful places around the world
Eats croissants in Paris, Stroopwaffle in Amsterdam
Has high tea in London, fresh pasta in Florence
Falls in and out of love easily
Always smiling without a care in the world
Does this girl even exist or is it all a facade?
A life curated just for social media
Warping my self-worth and killing my self-esteem
All for an unrealistic dream

THE PROCESS

5 Stages

There are five stages of grief
You start with denial
A shocking slap
Your situation is impossible
It feels like it's happening to someone else
A nightmare that you'll wake up from
eventually
You may not even shed a tear yet
This can't be happening
Next comes the anger
Your vision turns red
This happened to you
Because of someone else
You seethe at the injustice
Yell, scream and punch the wall
How could this be happening to me?
Slowly the anger fades
You begin to miss what you had
If you haven't already
You'll do anything to get it back
Lost in the *if only*
Bargaining has begun
Tell yourself that it can work out
If these conditions are met
All will be fine
You just need to talk to them
You're one conversation from fixed
Then you can go back to normal
You don't want to give up
Hold on, it's not over yet

Once they stop calling
You stop texting
The darkness starts seeping in
Depression settles and takes over
You realize that this new state is permanent
Your nightmare is reality
No more false hope
How will I get through this?
Day by day you prove your strength
You take little victories
Moving from the couch
Going a day without tears
You realize that the show must go on
The blackness dulls into grey
Slowly fading away
And you become a new version of yourself
You may not be the same
Not on the inside
But you learn to be okay on your own
Accepting your circumstance
I am all I need

Love Ending

Love is a deadly game
The life you built together, one day shatters
You're left to bury the remains
Say goodbye to a shared future

Pack your bags and shut the door
Only to never open it again
The last look, last hug, last kiss
Forever burned into your memory

Suddenly alone with your memories and thoughts
Pushing away the haunting ghost popping up unwanted
They don't just disappear
Endless reminders linger behind

You delete the picture and texts and, donate the gifts
Hesitated to delete their number, just in case
No matter how much you delete, they never go away
They dance in and out of your dreams

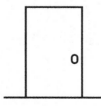

If you were in deep enough
There are even more loose ends
Shared friends you must split
Their family you will never see again

So much love lost
Holidays won't be the same for a while
A piece will be missing
An empty chair at the table

A cold hand that itches to be held
You're no longer yourself
A gaping hole you can't fill
No matter how much you try

Take it day by day
Hoping that one day the sun will shine again
Your smile will be genuine
You'll go a day without thinking of them

When you look back, just painless memories
Maybe another will take their spot
It can never be the same, but you're okay with that
You've learned to fill your own cup

Grieving

The stages of grief aren't a flow chart
You may eat breakfast in anger
Dine with depression
One day you're stuck in your worst nightmare
Another you feel okay and accepting
The emotions wash over you
But they're not always linear
You mood shifts from moment to moment
Triggers find you everywhere you go
Just when you feel okay
You're hit with a rogue memory
One you had forgotten
The tears start to fall without your consent
You end up running out of a store because of the
music
Stumble upon a picture, seeing their face
Acceptance replaced by bargaining
You'd do anything to get them back
The feeling fades and you're fine again
Grief's stages aren't mile markers
You move forward and back
Taking it day by day
Knowing one day you'll be okay
Even if it doesn't feel like it
Forgiving yourself for sliding back
Grabbing a tissue and riding out the waves
There's no way out, just through
Eventually, you come out stronger than ever
Armed with the knowledge that you survived

Death of a Relationship

How do you cope with the death of a relationship
Mourn the life you could have had together
Accept that you no longer are in each other's lives

Each day I have to let go of the life I wanted
The one I saw so clearly with you
And start planning alone

Would it be easier if you had died?
Instead, you're out there somewhere
Each day deciding you're better off without me

How am I supposed to let go?
Accept that it's really over
There's no going back

I have no power
It was one-sided
This isn't what I want

You gave up on me, on us
Decided I wasn't what you wanted
It didn't matter what I thought

Mourning

When you've built a life with someone
A breakup is like a death
But there's no body to mourn
You have to live every single day
Knowing they're very much alive
Living every day choosing not to call
Happily living a life without you
People don't respect your sadness
Expect you to quickly move on
Everyone goes through it, right?
It's just a breakup
But it's not that simple
It's the death of a relationship
I'm mourning the life we had together
The future I wanted and can never have
They expect me to get over it
But how can I?

I've trained my brain for years to think of you
You were my best friend
I thought you were my person
Now you're no one to me
Just another stranger
Can't call or text
I don't where you are or what you're doing
Have you replaced me yet?
What is she like? Why her?
How come it couldn't have been me?
You'll get married and have kids
All with someone else
She'll have the life I wanted with you
And I'm supposed to be "okay?"
Can't they see what I've lost
How hard I'm trying?
I am living in so much pain
But I hide it behind a smile
So I must be over it right?
Not even a little

The Aftermath

In the mirror, I see a face
Sad eyes and pale skin
Unwashed hair that's a bit too long
Wrinkled clothes with muted colors
Hunched shoulders and thin arms
A heartbroken stranger
I no longer recognize
Once full of smiles, laughter, and love
Now just the empty shell
Going through the motions
Alive, but not living

DENIAL

Time

At first, they said just give it time
The pain would dull
My heart would heal
Just take it day by day
Try to live in the moment
As the days, weeks, months go by
I cry less, but it still hurts
I still think of you
Every. Single. Day.
But I don't call or text
Is it easier? Not really
I don't miss you any less
I'm still struggling to get by
Trying to come to terms with reality
I've gotten better at hiding it
And I'm now used to the pain
Postpone the tears until I'm alone
The triggers come out of nowhere
I see you everywhere I go
My heart still aches for you
How did we get here?
When I look back it seems impossible
Yet here I am alone, without you
Dreaming of your face

Reality Check

It's hard for me to wrap my head around reality
The person I once trusted unconditionally
Is now a stranger to me
I told you all of my secrets
All of my inner thoughts
Did you not tell me yours?
You're the person I wanted to be with
My favorite companion
Now someone I can no longer call mine
I have no right to call you at all
Even speaking your name feels foolish
Letters my fingers naturally go to type
You feel like a distant dream
One that I can't quite grasp
Your face a little fuzzy
I can no longer remember every freckle
My daily life is a waking nightmare
One that I never wished for
Did our life together never happen?
Some days it feels that way

You were someone I made up in my head
We never walked the streets of London
Held hands in the rain in Rome
Kissed under the Paris lights
Got lost in Barcelona
Walked until our feet hurt in New York
How could all that have happened?
If I don't even know where you live
Where you work
What you're doing right now
I must have made it up
All of the pictures are gone
Any momentos hidden
All I'm left with are memories
And they feel fabricated
There's no way I could have lost so much
Had everything I wanted
All for it to disappear
It must have been a beautiful dream
One that I'll remember forever

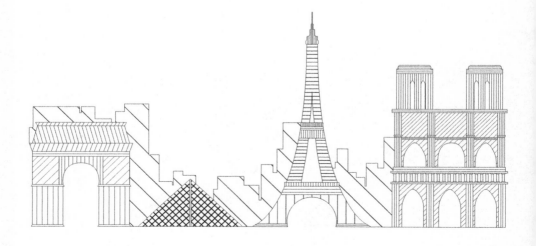

Warning Signs

I see other couples walking hand and hand
The girl looks blissfully happy as I once was
I see myself in her, you in him
I want to warn her
Tell her what can happen
Ask her if she has a backup plan
Let her know that she's not safe
The life they planned together
Could come crashing down

He could choose to walk away
It might not be a fight
There may not be a long buildup
One day he could just snap
And it will all be meaningless
The future they had suddenly dissipates
Like a dream she can see but no longer touch

Do you have any doubts?
Are you all-in?
Don't invest too much in one person
They'll only disappoint you
After they've greedily taken all you've given
Leave you empty and wondering
Where did it all go wrong?
But you'll never have the answer
You'll drive yourself crazy with your own thoughts
Theories and possibilities that have no endgame
One day you'll realize that there is no point

You think you know someone
But you don't know what's inside their head
The pieces they keep from you
Their deepest desires, their darkest thoughts
The person you share a life with one day could be
a stranger
You would walk past them on the street
Never knowing they were close enough to touch

Are you already in too deep like I was?
Is it too late for you to shield your heart?
Maybe you too are destined to fall and break
Even if I could tell you the ending
You wouldn't believe me
You'd choose your love, the inevitable pain
Because we're all addicts, love our drug of choice
We'll cling to it until we're left with no other
option
Until the other person closes and locks the door
Without giving us the spare key

You'll put your faith in him, just like I did
Against the odds and the statistics
Hopefully, you have people to pick up the pieces
Or maybe you're stronger than me
You could be the hammer and not the nail
I was a glass nail put up against a sledgehammer
I had no choice but to shatter
You may be a diamond
And I could have the story all wrong

Relentless Thoughts

Sometimes I think I can't go on
The pain weighs too much
I'm not strong enough to lift it
But I put on my smile
And keep on moving
Going through my routine
Wondering through every step
How did I get here?
Why haven't you come back?
I repeat questions that have no answers
Over and over again
Driving myself crazy

Therapy

I can no longer talk to you
No more texts, phone calls, or emails
I can't hug you or kiss you anymore
After deleting the photos and videos
All I can do is talk about you
Reminisce about the good times
Obsess over the bad
Replaying the last conversation over and over
Watch you walk out the door
Like a horror movie on repeat
I have to pay someone to listen
An hour a week to get out the pain
To talk about you with love, anger, and pain
She calms me through the same conversations
Fears and thoughts I have to voice again and again
How will I be happy again
I don't understand what went wrong
This isn't him
I can't let him go
We were different
Maybe he'll change his mind
She reassures me my feelings are normal
Promises me I will feel better one day
It happens to everyone she says
I thought our situation was special
Turns out it's the same story as everyone else
I just wasn't prepared for the ending

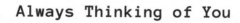

Always Thinking of You

My brain is programmed to think about you
Years of training don't just go away
No matter how much I try
How many times I redirect to anything else
Every memory cuts deep
Too many smiles and laughs
I look hard to find the cracks
Wondering what I missed
Changes I could have made
It's hard to not look you up
One smiling picture a wound to my soul
How are you smiling while I'm struggling so hard?
Who's taking the picture?
What does she look like?
Are you happier without me?
Would I even recognize you on the street?
I think about what I would say if you called
Dangerous thoughts that feed my addiction
These fantasies are my darkest vice
Feeding the demon that can't let go

Asleep

For a split second I think
You could appear out of thin air
Arms reached out for an embrace
Then I remember you're not here
I have no idea where you are
You decided you wanted out
We haven't spoken in months
I still look for you on the streets
My heart occasionally skipping
When someone reminds me of you
How long will I hold on
Wishing you'd show up
Fantasizing what I'd say
What it would take to make it work
I itch to call you up
I just want to hear your voice
My cheeks turn red and flushed
Embarrassment creeps in
You don't want me anymore
If you did, you'd call
You're going to move on
If you haven't already
But I'm stuck in the past
Terrified I can't move forward
Not knowing how to accept it
It still feels like a nightmare
After all of these months
I keep waiting to wake up
But I never do

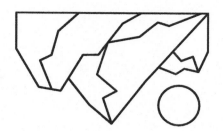

Lost

I built my life around you
When you left, I fell apart
My life unraveled in an instant
Spinning around without a center
You were my compass
Now I don't know where to go
Which way is North
What to do or who I am
I had everything I wanted
And I lost it so easily
I'm no longer me
I fake a smile and a laugh
Pretend that I'm okay
But I'm not

Sailor

I could do anything with you by my side
Your absence took away my wind
My sails hang lifeless
I'm stuck in the middle of the ocean
Alone and isolated
I've been turned around
Unable to see the shore
I try to row with my paddles
But my arms lack the strength
I needed you more than I let on
How do I navigate this alone?
You were supposed to be my partner
Life is a ship that takes two to steer

ANGER

Unfair

The next day I woke up
I wasn't in my bed
You weren't by my side
Yet the sun was still shining
How is that allowed?
Life should have stopped
How could everyone keep going on
Acting so normal
When my life just fell apart
Couldn't they feel the injustice
The mistake the universe just made

The Egomaniac

You look for girls who are broken
Becoming their knight in shining armor
Wanting to be their everything
Putting back their pieces
Weaving your way into their life
Until they can't manage without you
You've become their everything
Best friend, therapist, and partner
All wrapped into one
But as they get stronger, you get bored
And you start looking for your next project
Moving on, you take the supporting beam
And their whole world collapses
But you're not around to see it
Too busy cleaning up someone else's mess
Not the one you created
You're addicted to being needed
Feeling important and wanted
It feeds your self-esteem and precious ego

Alone

You weren't happy with your life
Used process of elimination
To figure out the cause
Trim away the excess fat
Little by little stripped it away
You decided I was the problem
I thought I was the solution
So easily you cut me away
Never looking back or apologizing
You wanted to be alone
To "figure things out"
Alone has a pretty face
And a nice body
Maybe she can fix you

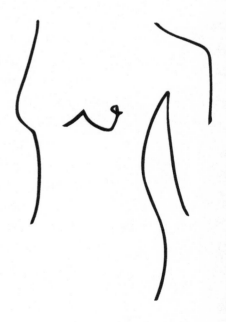

Darkest Thoughts

Sometimes I wish you were dead
So I could let go of this false hope
Stop wondering if you'll come back
And finally, move on

Don't

Don't tell me everything happens for a reason
I don't believe you right now
Don't list my ex's flaws
I still love them
Don't tell me I'll be better off
I miss them more than you know
Don't tell me they weren't right for me
I still want them
Don't tell me I'll find someone better
I think they're the best
Don't make me talk about it
I'll bring it up when I want to
Don't tell me they'll realize their mistake
I can't handle any more false hope
Don't tell me I need to get out there
I see their face in everyone I meet
Don't tell me when I should feel better
I heal at my own rate
Don't make me feel bad for still crying
I am mourning the life we could have had together
Don't tell me what they're up to
I can't handle knowing

Freed

You wanted freedom
I wanted a ring
My finger is bare
And you're nowhere to be found

Fate

I don't believe in fate
Or what's meant to be
It absolves you of fault
An easy way out
As if our choices don't matter
It was all predetermined
Marginalizing anger, relieving guilt
We're but pawns in a larger game
Trying to give our lives greater meaning
Instead, I believe in actions and decisions
You didn't have to leave me, you made a choice
I don't think it's because
There's someone better out there for me
When I eventually move on and find someone else
I'm told to be thankful for you
This is what needed to happen
I disagree, just as easily it could have been you
Believing in fate is so much easier
Then I'm better off without you
But I can't accept that
I've walked in both yards
One grass is much greener

The Game

You won and I lost
Two opponents in a game
But I didn't know I was playing
I thought we were on the same team
Turns out you only play solo
Take the winnings for yourself
And move on to the next match

BARGAINING

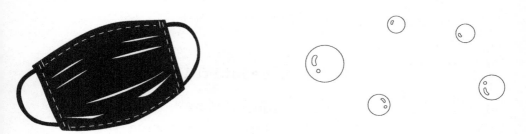

Quarantine

The world feels like it's ending
Streets are empty, shops bare and closed
You were supposed to be my survival partner
It would be us against the world
As long as we were together
I knew it would be alright
You are the only person
I want to be quarantined with
I'd give anything to be stuck inside with you
Unable to leave our little apartment
You, me, and our dog
The people we used to be
Ordering takeout and watching Netflix
I'd curl up against you on the couch
Hold your hand in mine
Wiggle my toes against yours
The dog curled by our feet
Locked in our own bubble
Where nothing else exists
I'd stay in this loop forever

The Most Beautiful Nightmare

Last night I dreamt of you
Your lips touched mine
I finally was able to release my breath
I've been holding it for months
You wrapped your arms around me
My hands explored your body in awe
I felt the muscles under your shirt
When I looked up at you
Your face was crystal clear
After all this time, I remember every detail
It's going to feel worse when I wake up
I whispered to you
I know, you apologized
I felt myself coming to
Holding on with all my strength
I clung to you
Let me stay in this dream forever
Don't make me say goodbye again
Slowly you faded away
When I finally opened my eyes
You weren't there
I closed my eyes and lay still
Willing myself back into the dream
Tears filled my eyes in defeat
These tortured dreams are all I have left
The closest I will ever get to you

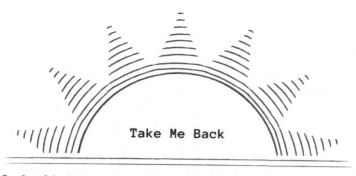

Take Me Back

I don't know what it will take to be happy
All I want is you, even now
I tell myself you'll come around
It's the saddest thing in the world
Because I know it isn't true
But it's a comforting thought
One that helps me get through the day
If you wanted me, you'd be here
You'd text or you'd call
Leave a breadcrumb trail
I dream of you every night
Wishing you'd come back
Bargaining with the universe
Thinking what I'd give up
How I would be different
It's a sick desperate spiral
I grasp onto every bit of false hope
I want you to make it better
Erase all of the pain
Take me back to the beginning
When it was all so easy and simple
Let me get lost in your love
Drown in your eyes
Reach out and take your hand
Walk into the sunset
Pretending it never happened
And do it all over again

Domestic Bliss

The littlest things remind me of you
Mundane moments that cut to my core
All of the stupid arguments
Which seemed so important at the time
Are now embarrassingly irrelevant
What I wouldn't give to battle it out with you
Have an argument over something simple
I'd let you win with a smile
See your dish left in the sink
Laundry crumpled and unfolded
Debate what to eat for dinner
Which new show to watch on tv
Enjoy every minute of it
I'd watch you while you sleep
Hold your hand every chance I got
Cling to you with all of my might
Because I know now what I'm missing

Imaginary Friend

I look around at my life today
This makes sense, I think
When I comb through my memories
The years we spent together
All of the adventures and love
Feel like a distant dream
I made it all up in my head
Of course, you're not here
You never existed at all
Just a figment of my imagination
I created the perfect daydream
In this fantasy, I had it all
The perfect life for just a few sweet minutes
But now I'm awake and empty
Wishing I could go back to sleep
Just to see your face again

Ghost

I even allowed to miss you still?
I'm holding onto a ghost
When I reach out, my hand passes through
You grin and fade away
I'm left smiling back at nothing
Haunted by what could have been

Temptation

Some days all I want is to hear you voice
Even if it will cause me pain
I want to pick up the phone
Dial your number
Hold my breath as you speak my name
The most beautiful sound in the world

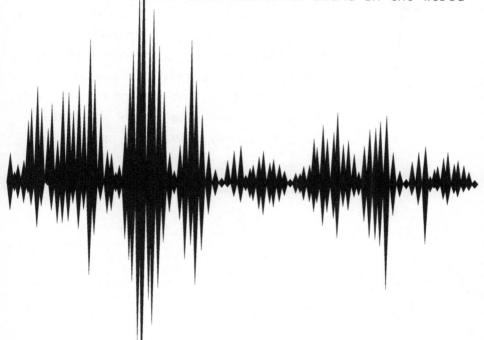

Holding On

We spent every day for years together
Now I can't even send you a text
You were the person I felt closest to
Yet you walked away so easily
When I think of never seeing you again
My stomach turns to ice
Panic runs through my veins
I can't do this without you
I need you
I'm not strong enough
This isn't real
I can't give up on us
But there's no other choice
I can't force you to love me
Every day I work so hard to keep moving
To rebuild a life without you
Tell myself that it's over
You're never coming back
But I still have trouble believing it
Despite not talking in months
I can't let you go
I compare everyone I meet to you
And they never add up

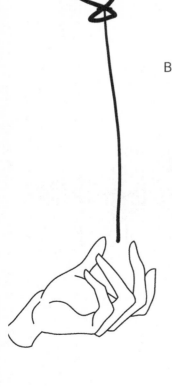

Wishful Thinking

There's a difference between wish and hope
My brain knows you're not going to call
But I still wish that you would
I've given up on the false hope
You would have changed your mind by now
It doesn't mean I don't still wish you would
More than anything in the world

Seconds of Bliss

There are moments when I forget
Just for a few seconds
Everything I lost
Why I'm here and not there
Then it hits
My stomach drops
I remember you're gone
And probably not coming back
Flashes of the nightmare
Every final word you said
How you looked when you walked away
My heart breaks again and again

DEPRESSION

Dreaming of Sunshine

The fog rolled in quickly
An opaque gloom absorbing the light
Occasionally the sun penetrates the dark clouds
For a minute I feel hopeful
Bathing in the warmth
The sunshine is brief but glorious
A welcomed break from the downpour
I'm trying to accept the bad weather
Wear my rain boots and carry an umbrella
Wait it out until it passes
I hold on to daydreams of clear skies
And cool breezes
Hoping I can go back to who I was before
The girl before the storm

Sad Heart

Sometimes my heart burns from missing you
I try not to think about who we were
What we had together
Now and then I fail
I'm sure you do too
I don't think I'll ever understand what happened
Why you chose to walk away
Leave everything we built behind
For what? Someone new or just something different
How many of your smiles were fake?
Covering up the doubting thoughts you had
I thought I knew you
Now I don't think I even scratched the surface
The person I saw wasn't capable of this
I went all in and made a bad bet
Believed the bluff with stars in my eyes
Now I guess you're someone else's
You'll hold and kiss them as you did me
Your face will be the first thing they see in the morning
I thought I'd wake up to you forever
Sleep by your side until our skin became wrinkled
Now you go to sleep next to someone else
I still sleep alone, not ready to replace you
Dreaming of you every night

Grey Glasses

Now the world seems dark and unforgiving
The sunlight stolen from the sky
No more light to pave the way
There are a million reasons to be unhappy

Skepticism and pessimism the reigning thoughts
Humanity is a lost cause
How do other people smile
Knowing the world is unfair and cruel

Each day they wake up, forgetting yesterday's struggles
I was once one of those people
Swapped my rose glasses for grey against my will
All the color drained from the world

Unfitting

I never fit just right
Like a shirt that's too loose and unflattering
Pants that are too tight and constraining
I know how to play the role
When to smile, laugh, what to say
But it all feels superficial and forced
Never perfectly at ease
Surrounded by those who don't seem to understand
Alone and wandering, wondering if it's me
An entire predicament dreamt up in my head
Neverending commentary from the inner critic
I'm unable to separate fact from fiction
Believing the story I wrote
The author of my loneliness and shame

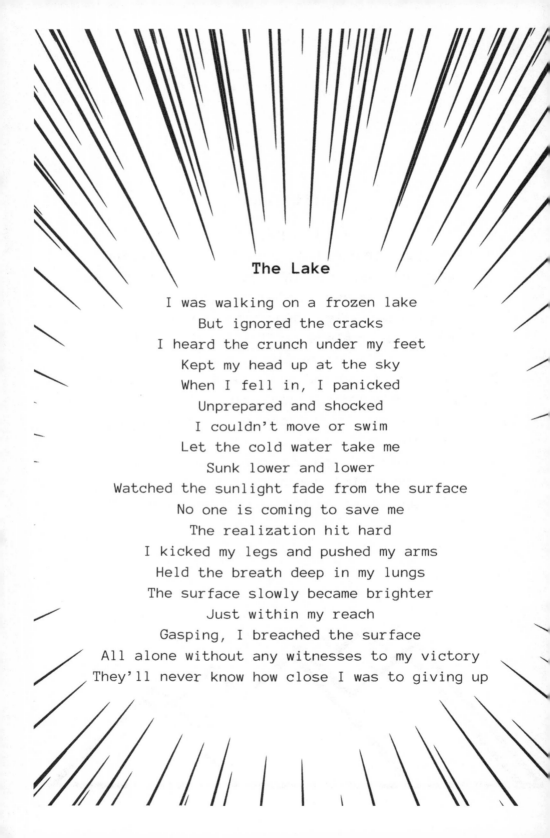

The Lake

I was walking on a frozen lake
But ignored the cracks
I heard the crunch under my feet
Kept my head up at the sky
When I fell in, I panicked
Unprepared and shocked
I couldn't move or swim
Let the cold water take me
Sunk lower and lower
Watched the sunlight fade from the surface
No one is coming to save me
The realization hit hard
I kicked my legs and pushed my arms
Held the breath deep in my lungs
The surface slowly became brighter
Just within my reach
Gasping, I breached the surface
All alone without any witnesses to my victory
They'll never know how close I was to giving up

Fake Happy

I only exist behind the screen
Living vicariously through the adventures of others
Scrolling past pictures of smiling faces
Remembering I was just like them
Posting snapshots of my life
Feeding off the likes and comments
Now there's no point
Nothing to show
I could pretend to be happy
Create false trips with fake laughs
Curating the life I wish I had
Is that what everyone else is doing?
Fabrications and manipulations
All meant to impress
Leaving us empty and shallow
Fueled by inconsequential numbers
To calculate our value
So busy capturing the moment
Distorting the truth
We forget how to live in the moment
And enjoy its beauty

Paradox

Somehow I feel both underwhelmed and overwhelmed
Too tired to move, yet needing to run
Paralyzed with anxiety, longing, and disappointment
Full of potential I'm unable to access
I quickly fill my to-do lists
But have no motivation to get started
One half says stop
The other says go
I'm itching for stimulation
Yet, annoyed by the commotion
The life I want looks nothing like
The one I live

Deepest Fear

I am a medium person
Unimpressively average
Always stuck right in the middle
Okay in everything that I do
Never terrible, never great
Destined to live a medium life

Uncinematic

TThe faces behind the screens
Feel more real than the ones in front of me
Everyday life is boring and bland
Lacking color and surprise
Reality moves at a slower speed
Lacking the cinematic moments
And beautifully scripted scenes
Capturing orchestrated happiness
The real world is unbearably dull
My life cannot compare
I have an insatiable craving for more
Unrealistic expectations
That slowly drive me insane

ACCEPTANCE

Empathy

Empathy is often confused with sympathy
I thought I lived vicariously
Through my favorite characters
I felt their loss, their pain, their suffering
Lead many lives through books and movies
When I saw my friend's hearts break
I comforted them in the best way I could
As tears streamed down their face
I thought I understood their pain

One day it happened to me
I unearthed a whole new level of compassion
What I thought was empathy, was just sympathy
You can't be empathetic
Until you've felt the agony yourself
Once you've had your heartbroken
Into a million little pieces
Too small to put back together right away
You have no idea what they're going through
The depths of their pain
How much you can miss someone

I now know I said all of the wrong things
Because I've heard them through wounded ears
The songs hit differently on the radio
I recognize the pain in others
My fellow warriors who have no choice
The world doesn't stop for you
You have to keep going
Each day the sun rises and sets
And you have to put one foot in front of the other

Happy Six Month Break Up Anniversary

Six months ago today
My heart shattered into a million pieces
I wrote you a note
Poured out my heart
You were my person, I was all in
Instead of the reassurance I craved, you let me go
You wanted love the way I loved you
You said you needed to be free
Change who you were
You didn't like the picture we were painting
You needed to paint something new
With someone else
I wasn't what you needed in a partner
Blamed all of your problems on me
Your reasons didn't make sense
It felt like a bad dream
The world turned upside down
All I could do was try to breathe
As tears streamed down my face
You held me, your face dry
I held your face and gave you one last kiss
I packed a bag as you took a bath
Grabbing the first things I touched
Sobbing uncontrollably, without anger
Overwhelmed with rejection and shock
I called my parents and let them know
Silent shock on the other line
My brother came to pick me up
You couldn't bear to see his face
You said goodbye to our dog
Broke both of our hearts
And walked out the door
You didn't look back

Be Mine

I yearn to be carefree
Falling in and out of love often
Collecting only shallow scratches
Laughing without pain
Living just below surface
Like a bee moving from flower to flower
Never staying for too long
Flying away without a dramatic exit
Instead, I jump right in
Diving fast and deep
Attaching myself to the flower
Holding on until it has to grow thorns
Shaking me off with devestating force
I have deep scars from my wounds
My wings are tattered, colors less bright
Weary from my travels
Yet, unable to resist a dangerously
pretty flower

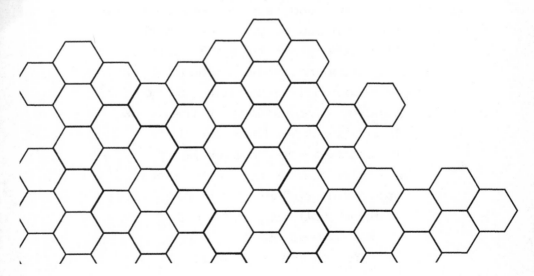

February 1st

It's your birthday today
And I can't even say "Happy Birthday"
For the first time in 7 years
I won't be lighting the candle
Reminding you to make your wish
I didn't make cinnamon rolls this morning
I haven't been shopping for the perfect gift
Any contact would show my desperation
You'd probably feel sorry for me
Kindly remind me that it's over
Tell me you've moved on
Or would you just say thank you
Smile at your phone wherever you are
You have to know I remember
After all those years I couldn't forget
I whisper "Happy Birthday" in my head
And wonder what you're doing
How you're spending your day
Who you're celebrating with
How many times you've thought of me
This time next year, will I still be thinking of you?
Will your birthday pass unnoticed
I'm not sure which thought is sadder

Waiting

How long before I stop checking my phone?
Expecting your name to turn up
The beautiful letters I once loved to say
Now spell out a stranger
I used to feel on edge
Knowing the phone was going to ring
Every time I stepped away, holding my breath
Yet your name never appeared
After a while, the phone became the enemy
I hear phantom rings and dings
My stomach rolls and drops
If your name popped up, nothing good would follow
It's past the point of no return
Just insignificant transactions left
Or selfish apologies
I can't afford to hurt anymore
With a few more words you could break me again
And I've come too far to fall back
It's better to never hear from you at all
Then to have any more cuts on my heart
I've only roughly stitched it back together
The thread is thin and frayed
Say the right words and it'll snap altogether
Undoing the months of hard work I've spent sewing
Gathering the pieces and trying to fasten them back
It still beats despite the abuse
But it still doesn't sound the same
I'm not sure it ever will

Rewrite the Story

Throw away the fairytales
Rewire your brain
Detox your mind and accept reality
The only happily ever after you need is you
You can have love but on your own terms
You do not need a man, but you can want one
Turn the page and write your own story
One where you are the main character
Not the love interest
On an adventure to take over the world

Neutral

My realization as the months pass by
I can live without you, but I don't want to
I'd rather take on the world with you by my side
Everything looks different through lonely eyes
Once teeming with colorful, now painfully dull
Taking it day by day, I grow
Relishing the smallest victories
Claiming back my life, but it's not easy
I've been stuck in neutral
Hoping you'd change your mind
Completely powerless
Unable to move forward
I'm starting to realize I have no choice
You're not coming back
There's no one to wait for
I have to plan for my own future
One without you in it
Power through the pain
Even when it hurts just to breathe
Putting one foot in front of the other
Living each day knowing one day I'll feel better
Even if it's not today

ABOUT THE AUTHOR

Lynn Moore is a writer that uses her real-life experiences and taps into shared emotions like grief and depression when creating. She has a bachelor's in psychology and a master's degree in communications. Solidarity is her debut book.

You can follow her at @CupOfTeaPoetry on Instagram.

Solidarity is a collection of poems that explore grief and heartbreak. These poems speak to your pain and help you to feel less alone during your darkest times. Solidarity turns pain into beauty, putting into words the agony, uncertainty, anxiety, and defeat that comes with loss.

My Curse

Once I open my heart
It never fully shuts
I've tried tape, glue, and thread
Nothing can keep it closed
Bits of love always shine through
Never forgetting, unable to redirect
A short list of names
Forever tattooed on my soul

Made in the USA
Monee, IL
01 December 2022

18888400R00049